Be happy.

Remember to live, love, laugh and learn.

Compiled by Dan Zadra

Designed by Kobi Yamada and Steve Potter

COM·PEN´·DI·UM™
Publishing

Enriching the lives of millions, one person at a time.™

Acknowledgements

These quotations were gathered lovingly but unscientifically over several years and/or contributed by many friends or acquaintances. Some arrived—and survived in our files—on scraps of paper and may therefore be imperfectly worded or attributed. To the authors, contributors and original sources, our thanks, and where appropriate, our apologies. —The Editors

With Special Thanks To

Jason Aldrich, Gerry Baird, Jay Baird, Neil Beaton, Doug Cruickshank, Jim Darragh, Kari Cassidy-Diercks, Kyle Diercks, Josie and Rob Estes, Jennifer Hurwitz, Liam Lavery, Connie McMartin, Cristal & Brad Olberg, Janet Potter & Family, Diane Roger, Aimee Rawlins, Sam Sundquist, Jenica Wilkie, Heidi Wills, Robert & Val Yamada, Justi, Tote & Caden Yamada, Kaz & Kristin Yamada, Tai & Joy Yamada, Anne Zadra, and August & Arline Zadra

Credits

Compiled by Dan Zadra
Designed by Kobi Yamada and Steve Potter

Printed in Hong Kong

CONTENTS

Live,

Love,

Laugh

& Learn

Happiness Lies in Wait

I once read an article about a crowded little island. It turns out that everyone in the world, including you and me, has visited this destination several times. The island is called the *Someday I'll*—and many people who go there never return:

"Someday I'll get my driver's license, and then I'll be happy. Someday I'll graduate from college, and then I'll be happy. Someday I'll have a wonderful job, family, house, dog and boat, and then I'll be happy. Someday I'll retire and—just you wait and see—I'll really be happy then."

Life on the *Someday I'll* isn't so bad. To be honest, I often find myself washed up on those dreamy shores. It's a peaceful, stress-free little place; there's usually something "just around the corner" to look forward to; and every tomorrow always promises to be better than today.

The problem, of course, is that tomorrow is promised to no one, and today is really the only day we have. As one of the quotes in these pages reminds us, "Begin doing what you want to do now. We are not living in eternity. We have only this moment, sparkling like a star in our hand—and melting like a snowflake."

If there's another message in this book it's probably this: Happiness is not so much a distant destination or a prized possession—it's more a matter of personal choice, or a way of traveling. Not just someday, but each and every day offers endless opportunities to live, love, laugh and learn—to open our arms and let it all in—and to share the day with those we love. It's in these everyday moments, both large and small, that happiness lies in wait.

Dan Zadra

What is life for? It is for you! Life must be lived, that's all there is to it. And a good time to live is any time you can. Today is the gift you may wish you had back tomorrow. So open your arms

Live, Love, I

and take it all in. This is your moment; this is your time for adventure, risk and living. Truly you will never have this opportunity again. Everything is a once-in-a-lifetime experience.

augh & Learn

Be happy.

Why wait? Life is not a dress
rehearsal. Quit practicing what
you're going to do, and just do it. In one
bold stroke you can transform today.
—Phillip Markins

Have a go. Anybody can do it.
—Alan Parker

The first step towards getting
somewhere is to decide that you are
not going to stay where you are.
—J. Pierpont Morgan

Live, Love, L

Let us live while we live.

—Philip Doddridge

The best day of your life is
the one on which you decide your life
is your own. No apologies or excuses.
No one to lean on, rely on, or blame.
The gift of life is yours; it is an
amazing journey; and you alone are
responsible for the quality of it.

—Dan Zadra

Make each day your masterpiece.

—John Wooden

augh & Learn

Life is in the here and now.
Either we meet it, we live it—or we miss it.
—Vimala Thakar

Seek and you will find. Don't be
willing to accept an ordinary life.
—Salle Merrill Redfield

Day after day, we discover our own lives.
Because we never know what we will find,
every discovery is an unexpected
gift we give to ourselves.
—Barbara J. Esbensen

Live, Love, L

Life is ours
to be spent, not saved.
—D. H. Lawrence

We are here, and it is now.
What else is there?

—Kobi Yamada

That it will never come again
is what makes life so sweet.
—Emily Dickinson

augh & Learn

I have always been delighted
he prospect of a new day, a fresh try,
one more start, with perhaps a bit of magic
waiting somewhere behind the morning.
—J.B. Priestley

Oh, the experience of this sweet life.
—Dante

Never lose an opportunity of seeing
anything that is beautiful.
—Ralph Waldo Emerson

Live, Love, L

The aim of life is to live,
and to live means to be aware,
joyously, drunkenly, divinely aware.

—Henry Miller

I want to convince you that
you must learn to make every
moment count, since you are going
to be here for only a short while.

—Don Juan

These are the days
of miracle and wonder.

—Paul Simon

Living is doing.

—Clara Barton

Life, we learn too late,
is in the living, the tissue of
every day and hour.

—Stephen B. Leacooke

One thing we can't recycle
is wasted time.

—Unknown

Live, Love, L

The tragedy of life is not so much
what we suffer, but rather what we miss.

—Thomas Carlyle

We cannot put off living until we are
ready. The most salient characteristic
of life is its urgency, "here and now"
without any possible postponement.
Life is fired at us point-blank.

—Jose Ortega y Gasset

Tomorrow's life is too late.
Live today.

—Martial

Everything is a
once-in-a-lifetime experience.

—Kobi Yamada

Twenty years from now you
will be more disappointed by the things
you didn't do than by the ones you did do.
So throw off the bowlines, sail away from the
safe harbor. Catch the tradewinds in your
sails. Explore. Dream. Discover.

—Mark Twain

Do not delay; the golden moments fly!

—Henry Wadsworth Longfellow

Live, Love, L

Life is a succession of moments.
To live each one is to succeed.

—Corita Kent

Today a new sun rises for me;
everything lives, everything is
animated, everything seems to speak
to me of my passion, everything
invites me to cherish it.

—Anne de Lenclos

Today I don't want to live for,
I want to live.

—Hugh Prather

Say yes to life, even though
you know it may devour you.

—Stephen Larsen

Living is a form of not being sure,
not knowing what next or how.
The moment we know how, we begin
to die a little. We never entirely know.
We guess. We may be wrong, but we
take leap after leap in the dark.

—Agnes De Mille

Oh for a life of sensations
rather than of thoughts!

—John Keats

Live, Love, I

I would like to learn,
or remember, how to live.

—Annie Dillard

I wish that life should not
be cheap, but sacred. I wish the days
be as centuries, loaded, fragrant.

—Emerson

If one is forever cautious,
can one remain a human being?

—Aleksandr Solzhenitsyn

ugh & Learn

Taking chances helps you grow.
—Unknown

Never be afraid to ask a question,
especially of yourself—discovery is
the mission of life.
—Brian Kates

We fail far more often by
timidity than by over-daring.
—David Grayson

The policy of being
too cautious is the greatest risk of all.

—Jawaharlal Nehru

Safety is the most unsafe path
you can take, safety keeps you numb
and dead. People are caught by surprise
when it is time to die. They have allowed
themselves to live so little.

—Steven Levine

There's no such thing as "zero risk."

—William Driver

Unless you walk out into the unknown,
the odds of making a profound difference in
your life are pretty low.

—Tom Peters

Boredom arises from routine.
Joy, wonder, rapture, arise from surprise.

—Leo Buscaglia

Because of our routines we forget that life is
an ongoing adventure.

—Maya Angelou

Live, Love, L

Nothing ventured, something lost.
—Neale Clapp

If you wait for the perfect moment when
all is safe and assured, it may never arrive.
Mountains will not be climbed, races won,
or lasting happiness achieved.
—Maurice Chevalier

If you put everything off until you're sure
of it, you'll get nothing done.
—Norman Vincent Peale

The greatest mistake we can make is to be continually fearing that we will make one.

—Elbert Hubbard

Let your mind fly toward "what-if?" Let your what-if become "why-not?" Then you're on your way. Why not, when life is so short, and we are such grand people?

—Larsen & Hegarty

It is only in adventure that some people succeed in knowing themselves— in finding themselves.

—Andre Gide

Live, Love, L

Simply, the thing
that I am shall make me live.

—William Shakespeare

Every life comes with a story…
and a possibility for a great adventure.

—Kobi Yamada

We need to live life with
a burning passion. No fire,
no heat—no heat, no life.

—Rebecca Stuttelle

I would rather have
30 minutes of "wonderful"
than a lifetime of nothing special.

—Julia Roberts

Feel the fear and do it anyway.

—Susan Jeffers

Anything I've ever done
that ultimately was worthwhile…
initially scared me to death.

—Betty Bender

Live, Love, L

Great things are only possible
with outrageous requests.

—Thea Alexander

Chained by their attitudes,
they are a slave, they have
forfeited their freedom. Only a
person who risks is free.

—Unknown

Our doubts are traitors, and
make us lose the good we
oft might win by fearing the attempt.

—William Shakespeare

There's as much risk in doing
nothing as in doing something.

—Trammell Crow

There's a big difference between
seeing an opportunity and seizing
an opportunity.

—Jim Moore

Life is always walking up to us and saying,
"Come on in, the living's fine," and what
do we do? Back off and take its picture.

—Russell Baker

Live, Love, L

Do one thing every day
that scares you.

—Unknown

How many people do
you know who spend their lives
taxiing down the runway of life,
revving their engines, but afraid to
take off? We were all designed to fly!

—Dr. H. Paul Jacobi

Freedom lies in being bold.

—Robert Frost

You must take your chance.

—William Shakespeare

Life has its own
hidden forces which you can
only discover by living.

—Soren Kierkegaard

I'm a big believer in just
saying yes if someone asks you
if you can do something.

—Piper Perabo

Live, Love, L

Everyone needs and deserves
love and happiness. Let's not wait until
we're perfect to go out and find it.

—Pat A. Mitchell

Do not be too timid and squeamish about
your actions. All life is an experience.

—Ralph Waldo Emerson

Of all the forms of caution,
caution in love is perhaps the most
fatal to true happiness.

—Bertrand Russell

augh & Learn

Grab a chance and you
won't be sorry for a might have been.

—Arthur Ransome

As you grow older, you'll find
that the only things you regret
are the things you didn't do.

—Zachary Scott

This is my life; I'm not going to
have this moment again.

—Bernie Seigel

Live, Love, L

We don't have an eternity to realize
our dreams, only the time we are here.

—Susan King Taylor

History doesn't belong to
the best. It belongs to those
who want it the worst.

—Sam Sundquist

The days come and go, but
they say nothing, and if we do not
use the gifts they bring, they carry
them as silently away.

—Ralph Waldo Emerson

There are only
so many tomorrows.

—Michael Landon

Why do we put off
living the way we want to live,
as if we have all the time
in the world?

—Barbara de Angelis

There's less time left.

—Malcolm Forbes

Live, Love, I

Nobody can
experience our lives for us.

—Charlotte Joko Beck

Make your life a happy one.
That is where success is
possible to everyone.

—Robert Powell

We might as well live.

—Dorothy Parker

Fall in love with your life. Give yourself permission to have a magnificent obsession. Life is an amazing adventure. Have the courage to follow your passion wherever it may take you. Plead guilty and often

Live, Love, L

to loving your family and friends. If you want love, give it away, that's how it works; and where love is present, life is full. So, follow your life's loves to the end. Do whatever your heart leads you to do—but do it!

augh & Learn

Be happy.

Love is such a big word,
it really should have more letters.

—Kobi Yamada

Love is the single most
important aspect of life.

—John Robbins

A life spent loving...
is a life well-spent.

—Lipton Marta

Live, Love, L

In dreams and in love,
there are no impossibilities.

—Janos Arony

We can only learn to love by loving.

—Iris Murdock

Spread your love
everywhere you go.

—Mother Teresa

augh & Learn

I have a heart
with room for every joy.

—P.J. Bailey

I'm really convinced that if we
were to define love, the only word big
enough to engulf it all would be "life."
Love is life in all its aspects. And if
you miss love, you miss life.

—Leo Buscaglia

Open your mind, open your heart, open
your arms, take it all in.

—Kobi Yamada

Live, Love, L

It is safe to let the love in.
Love is your divine right.

—Louise L. Hay

In the human heart new
passions are forever being born;
the overthrow of one almost always
means the rise of another.

—La Rochefoucauld

Perhaps loving something
is the only starting place there is
for making your life your own.

—Alice Koller

Only love makes life meaningful.

—Anonymous

You must find the passion,
an unrelenting passion.

—David Easton

Only passions,
great passions, can elevate
the soul to great things.

—Denis Diderot

Live, Love, L

Follow what you love and it
will take you where you want to go.

—Natalie Goldberg

There are many things in life that will
catch your eye, but only a few will catch
your heart. Pursue these.

—Michael Nolan

The essential conditions of everything we
do must be choice, love, passion.

—Nadia Boulanger

augh & Learn

Unlock your natural desires
by doing what you enjoy.

—Hans Selye

You only lose energy when
life becomes dull in your mind.
You don't have to be tired and bored.
Get interested in something.
Get absolutely enthralled in something.
Throw yourself into it with abandon.

—Norman Vincent Peale

Fall in love with what you do; believe in it;
strive to continuously improve.

—Bob Moawad

Live, Love, L

Love, and do what you like.

—St. Augustine

I think people don't place
a high enough value on how much
they are nurtured by doing whatever
it is that totally absorbs them.

—Jean Shinoda Bolen, M.D.

Desire creates the power.

—Raymond Holliwell

Anything you're good at
contributes to happiness.

—Bertrand Russell

Don't worry about what the
world wants from you, worry about
what makes you come more alive.
Because what the world really needs
are people who are more alive.

—Lawrence Le Shan

If you follow your bliss, doors will
open for you that wouldn't have
opened for anyone else.

—Joseph Campbell

Failures are few among people
who have found a work they enjoy
enough to do it well. You invest time
in your work; invest love in it too.

—Clarence Flynn

High achievement requires an
emotional investment. Unfortunately,
there are scores of people who do not
make the investment—who do not
feel strongly about anything.

—Theodore Isaac Rubin

Be absolutely determined
to enjoy what you do.

—Gerry Sikorski

Know what you love and
do what you love. If you don't do what
you love, you're just wasting your time.

—Billy Joel

Everyone has been made for some
particular work and the desire for that
work has been put in his or her heart.

—Rumi

When you do not tire within but
seek the sweet satisfaction of your life
and your work, you are doing what you were
meant to be doing.

—Gary Zukav

48

Everyone should carefully observe
which way his heart draws him, and then
choose that way with all his strength.

—Hasidic Saying

To make a living is no longer enough.
Work also has to make a life.

—Peter Drucker

To love what you do and feel that it matters—
how could anything be more fun?

—Katharine Graham

Relationships create the
fabric of our lives. They are the
fibers that weave all things together.
—Eden Froust

Cherish your human connections:
your relationships with friends and family.
—Barbara Bush

People who love us for what we are,
not for what we have done,
are precious support when we're
trying to do and be more.
—Peter McWilliams

Live, Love, L

There are many compliments
that may come to an individual
in the course of a lifetime, but there
is no higher tribute than to be loved
by those who know us best.

—Dr. Dale E. Turner

People don't care how much you know
until they know how much you care.

—Mike McNight

The way is long—let us go together.
The way is difficult—let us help each
other. The way is joyful—let us share it.
The way is ours alone—let us go in love.

—Joyce Hunter

ugh & Learn

Friends feed each other's spirits and
dreams and hopes; they feed each other
with the things a soul needs to live.

—Glen Harrington-Hall

I think we're here for each other.

—Carol Burnett

Friends are angels who lift us
to our feet when our wings have
trouble remembering how to fly.

—Unknown

Live, Love, L

Ah! How good it feels,
the hand of an old friend.

—Longfellow

The warmth of a
friend's presence brings joy to
our hearts, sunlight to our souls,
and pleasure to all of life.

—Unknown

The best thing to
hold on to in life is each other.

—Audrey Hepburn

ugh & Learn

We need to think of ourselves
as gifts to be given and to think of
others as gifts offered to us.

—John Powell

Each friend represents a world
in us, a world possibly not born until
they arrive, and it is only by this
meeting that a new world is born.

—Anais Nin

Happiness is not so much
in having as in sharing.

—Ernie McBratney

Live, Love, I

Being deeply loved by someone
gives you strength, while loving
someone deeply gives you courage.

—Lao-Tzu

It would be a fine thing, in which I
hardly dare believe, to pass our lives near
each other, hypnotized by our dreams.

—Elie Smithsen

My lifetime listens to yours.

—Margaret Peters

Great thoughts
always come from the heart.

—Marquis de Vauvenargues

One good heart attracts another.
Each true friend deserves the other.

—Shaker Saying

Everywhere, we learn best from
those whom we love.

—Goethe

Live, Love, L

When you're with a friend,
your heart has come home.

—Emily Farrar

I have forged my own life,
but not alone; my friends have
made the better part of it.

—Shawna Corley

We are so much less
without each other.

—Leo Buscaglia

Love is the
whole and more than all.
—E.E. Cummings

Blessed is the
influence of one true,
loving human soul to another.
—George Eliot

Only connect.
—E.M. Forster

Live, Love, L

Loving can cost a lot;
not loving always costs more.

—Merle Shain

The more you love,
the more you are given
to love with.

—Lucien Price

Each of us has a choice about
how to love the world in our
unique way.

—Bernie Siegel, M.D.

We can live a life full
and complete, thinking with our
heads but living from our hearts.

—Helen Hunt, M.A.

The love we desire is already within us.

—A Course in Miracles

I believe that everyone, with absolutely
no exceptions, can give love and that one
single loving person changes the world.

—Barry Neil Kaufman

Live, Love, l

Love makes your soul crawl
from its hiding place.

—Zora Neale Hurston

We all have the power to give away love,
to love other people. And if we do so, we
change the kind of person we are, and we
change the kind of world we live in.

—Rabbi Harold Kushner

You have something to give.
Give it!

—Kobi Yamada

Any place that we love
becomes our world.

—Oscar Wilde

You have a unique message to deliver;
a unique song to sing, a unique act of
love to bestow. This message, this song,
and this act of love have been entrusted
exclusively to the one and only you.

—John Powell, S.J.

Live to shed joys on others.

—Henry Ward Beecher

Live, Love, I

There isn't any formula or method.
You learn to love by loving.
—Aldous Huxley

The loving are the daring.

—Bayard Taylor

Person to person, moment to moment,
as we love, we change the world.
—Samahria Lyte Kaufman

ugh & Learn

The conclusion is always
the same: love is the most powerful
and still the most unknown energy
of the world.

—Pierre Teilhard De Chardin

What we love and what captures
our curiosity draws us forward into
some place of great destiny.

—Wayne Muller

At some point your heart will
tell itself what to do.

—Achaan Chah

Live, Love, L

Love, remember,
comes from inside of us.
It's not something we wait to get.

—James and Salle Merrill Redfield

To live without loving is
not really to live.

—Moliere

And in the end, the love you take is
equal to the love you make.

—The Beatles

Live, Love, I

mile, laugh, howl and
joy—life is the celebra-
on and you're invited.
sense of humor is
sential for good health
d abundant living.
here is not one shred
evidence that life is
rious. It is something to
savored and

ugh & Learn

easured,
ther than endured.
bstacles come and
bstacles go, they are
mply there for us
learn and to grow.
look around, funny
ings are everywhere.
e less you laugh, the
ss you live.

Be happy.

Life is really fun,
if we only give it a chance.
—Tim Hansel

The most useless day is that in which
we have not laughed.
—Charles Field

Laughter is a celebration of
the human spirit.
—Sabina White

Live, Love, l

I am sincere about life,
but I'm not serious about it.

—Alan Watts

Laughter is by definition healthy.

—Doris Lessing

He who laughs, lasts.

—Mary Pettibone Poole

ugh & Learn

Happiness makes up in height
for what it lacks in length.

—Robert Frost

From there to here, and here to there,
funny things are everywhere.

—Dr. Seuss

Do something. If it doesn't
work, do something else.
Nothing is too crazy.

—Jim Hightower

Live, Love, L

Have fun…anything can change,
without warning, and that's why I try not to
take any of what's happened too seriously.

—Donald Trump

Each instant is a place
we've never been.

—Mark Strand

This is what it's all about: If you
can't have fun at it, there's no
sense hanging around.

—Joe Montana

Time for a little something.

—A. A. Milne

What the world really needs is
more love and less paperwork.

—Pearl Bailey

The time to laugh is when you
don't have time for it.

—Argus Poster

Live, Love, L

Happiness is nothing more than
good health and a poor memory.

—Albert Schweitzer

Laughing is the sensation of
feeling good all over and showing
it principally in one spot.

—Josh Billings

Fun is fundamental.

—Doug Hall

You grow up the day you have
your first real laugh—at yourself.

—Ethel Barrymore

74   Cherish forever what makes you unique,
'cuz you're really a yawn if it goes!

—Bette Midler

In life, each of us must sometime
play the fool.

—Yiddish saying

Live, Love, L

If you aren't making some mistakes,
you aren't taking enough chances.

—John Sculley

I'll match my flops with anybody's
but I wouldn't have missed them.
Flops are a part of life's menu and
I've never been one to miss out
on any of the courses.

—Rosalind Russell

If at first you don't succeed, find out
if the loser gets anything.

—Bill Lyon

Success will come to you in
direct proportion to the number of
times you are willing to risk failure.
—EDGE Keynote

No experiment is ever a complete failure.
It can always be used as a bad example.
—Paul Dickson

Experience is the comb life gives you
after you lose your hair.
—Judith Stearn

Live, Love, I

If you decide to take the plunge,
please return it by next Tuesday.
—Robin Williams

Learn from the mistakes of others—
you can't live long enough to make
them all yourself.
—Carlyle

If you're already walking on thin ice,
why not dance?
—Gil Atkinson

In the game of life it's a good idea
to have a few early losses, which relieves
you of the pressure of trying to maintain
an undefeated season.

—Bill Vaughan

To obtain maximum attention, it's
hard to beat a good, big mistake.

—David D. Hewitt

The value of being able to laugh at
ourselves when we make a mistake:
it helps us get on with our work.

—Ken Blanchard

Live, Love, L

Do everything.
One thing may turn out right.

—Humphrey Bogart

I think the next best thing to solving
a problem is finding some humor in it.

—Frank Clark

Better days are just around the corner.
They're called Saturday and Sunday.

—Frank Vizarre

You can't really be strong
until you see a funny side to things.

—Ken Kesey

If we're going to be able to look back
on something and laugh about it, we
might as well laugh about it now.

—Marie Osmond

Life is a rollercoaster. Try to eat
a light lunch.

—David A. Schmaltz

Live, Love, l

You win some and you learn some.

—Barry Johnson

Nothing is terminal, just transitional.

—Dr. Robert Schuller

To really enjoy the better things in life,
one must first have experienced
the things they are better than.

—Oscar Homoka

Life is like playing the
violin solo in public and learning
the instrument as you go along.

—Samuel Butler

There are enough tragedies in life;
we have to have some laughs.

—Steve Allen

Being able to laugh
got me through.

—Toni Morrison

Live, Love, I

Don't let yesterday
use up too much of today.

—Erma Phillips

A workable measure of your progress
is how fast you can get free when you
are stuck and how many ways you
know to get free.

—Kathlyn Hendricks

Success is failure turned inside out.

—Frank Tyger

Honestly face defeat; never fake success.
Exploit the failure; don't waste it.
Learn all you can from it. Never use
failure as an excuse for not trying again.
—Charles Kettering

84 When you get to the end of your rope,
tie a knot, hang on—and swing!
—Leo Buscaglia

Give the world the best that you have and
you may get kicked in the teeth. Give the
world the best that you have anyway.
—The Edge

Live, Love, I

If you could choose one
characteristic that would get you
through life, choose a sense of humor.

—Jennifer James

Do not take life too seriously;
you will never get out of it alive.

—Elbert Hubbard

Humor is a proof of faith.

—Charles M. Schulz

augh & Learn

A light heart lives long.

—William Shakespeare

I have a new philosophy:
I'm only going to dread
one day at a time.

—Charles Schulz

What I'm looking for is a blessing
that's not in disguise.

—Kitty O'Neill Collins

Live, Love, L

How can there be such a difference
between a day off and an off day?

—Dale Enrich

God always has another
custard pie up his sleeve.

—Lynn Redgrave

If you are having a bad day, get
another one and get it quick!

—Rissie Harris

Life isn't just the front page—
it's the comics, too.

—Jim Althoff

No sense being pessimistic.
It wouldn't work anyway!

—Graffito

Life is a lot more amusing
than we thought.

—Andrew Lang

Live, Love, L

There is always a time for
gratitude and new beginnings.

—J. Robert Moskin

On with the dance!
Let joy be unconfined.

—George Gordon, Lord Byron

Laughter prevents hardening
of the attitudes.

—Dunc Muncy

Smile—it's the second
best thing you can do with your lips.

—Don Ward

It takes 17 muscles to smile,
and 47 muscles to frown. Conserve energy.

—Unknown

Laughter is the best medicine
in the world.

—Milton Berle

Live, Love, L

I enjoy a good laugh—
one that rushes out of one's soul like
the breaking up of a Sunday School.

—Josh Billings

No symphony orchestra ever
played music like a two-year-old girl
laughing with a puppy.

—Bern Williams

Never lose your child's heart.

—Mencius

I don't know why we are here, but
I'm pretty sure it has something
to do with enjoying ourselves.
—Ludwig Wittgenstein

Let there be more joy and laughter
in your living.
—Eileen Caddy

Lots of laughter and a sprinkling of love—
as far as we know, that's the best
way to deal with anyone.
—Lynne Alpern and Esther Bumenfeld

Live, Love, L

Shared laughter creates a bond of friendship. When people laugh together, they cease to be young and old, teacher and pupils, worker and boss. They become a single group of human beings.

—W. Lee Grant

We cannot really love anybody with whom we never laugh.

—Agnes Repplier

The less you laugh, the less you live.

—Tote Yamada

We don't stop laughing because
we grow old—we grow old because
we stop laughing.

—Michael Pritchard

If you laugh a lot, when you get older
your wrinkles will be in the right places.

—Andrew Mason

I always knew I would look back at
the times I'd cried and laugh, but I
never knew that I'd look back at
the times I'd laughed and cry.

—Shaun Prowdzik

Live, Love, L

If you really want to be happy,
nobody can stop you.

—Sister Mary Tricky

Live nutty. Just occasionally.
Just once in a while. And see what
happens. It brightens up the day.

—Leo Buscaglia

Sit loosely in the saddle of life.

—Robert Louis Stevenson

ugh & Learn

Live, Love, L

The place to be happy
is here and the time to
be happy is now. In a
very real way, we are the
authors of our own lives.
We do not remember
days, we remember
moments. Life is the
journey—live your life
on purpose.

ugh & Learn

Every moment is a place
we've never been. Meet
today with expectation,
enthusiasm and surprise.
It's time to start living
the life you've imagined!

Be happy.

Fill your life with as many
moments and experiences of joy and
passion as you humanly can. Start with
one experience and build on it.

—Wieder Marcia

How shall we live?
Live welcoming all.

—Mechtild of Magdeburg

Where your pleasure is, there is
your treasure; where your treasure,
there your heart; where your heart,
there your happiness.

—Augustine

Live, Love, L

The grand essentials of happiness are:
something to do, something to love,
and something to hope for.

—Allan K. Chalmers

The time that gets wasted is the time you
don't spend in each moment, experiencing
and appreciating it for what it is.

—Barbara de Angelis

Life is a series of moments.
Each moment should be welcomed
in joy and relinquished in joy.

—Deepak Chopra

augh & Learn

Happiness comes of the capacity
to feel deeply, to enjoy simply, to think
freely, to risk life, to be needed.

—Storm Jameson

It seems obvious that the
first rule of life is to have a good time.

—Brendan Gill

The place to be happy is here.
The time to be happy is now.
The way to be happy is to make others so.

—Robert G. Ingersoll

Live, Love, L

Savor the moment. Search for a
little joy, and you will find a great
deal of it in unexpected places.

—Allen Folstein

The point is to live everything.

—Steven Potter

People will try to tell you that all
the great opportunities have been
snapped up. In reality, the world changes
every second, blowing new opportunities
in all directions, including yours.

—Ken Hakuta

Life is a succession of lessons which
must be lived in order to be understood.
—Ralph Waldo Emerson

Life needs to be lived in a
constant state of discovery.
—Kobi Yamada

We can learn nothing except by going
from the known to the unknown.
—Claude Bernard

Live, Love, l

The main point in the game of life
is to have fun. We are afraid to have fun
because somehow that makes life too easy.

—Sammy Davis, Jr.

There are only two things you
"have to" do in life. You "have to" die
and you "have to" live until you die.
You make up all the rest.

—Marilyn Grey

As I grow to understand life less and less,
I learn to love it more and more.

—Jules Renard

Develop interest in life as you see it;
in people, things, literature, music—the
world is so rich, simply throbbing with
rich treasures, beautiful souls and
interesting people. Forget yourself.

—Henry Miller

Learning something new is
the bestest thing in the world.

—Andrew Harper, Age 7

One of the most wonderful things about
life is that there's always so much more
to know, so much more to discover.

—Joni Eareckson Tada

Live, Love, L

I think everything has value, absolute
value; a child, a house, a day's work, the sky.
But nothing will save us. We were never
meant to be saved. What were we meant
for then? To love the whole damned world.

—Jane Rule

Love really is the answer. We're here
only to teach love. When we're doing that,
our souls are singing and dancing.

—Gerald Jampolsky, M.D.

It seems to me we can never
give up longing and wishing while we
are thoroughly alive. There are certain
things we feel to be beautiful and good,
and we must hunger after them.

—George Eliot

Between the wish
and the thing, life lies waiting.
—Unknown

Your mind must remain open
at all times. If you do not expect
the unexpected, you will not find it.
—Heraclitus

Life never becomes a habit to me.
It's always a marvel.
—Katherine Mansfield

Live, Love, L

May your mind forever
sparkle like a star, your heart remain
pure as new fallen snow, and your spirit
forever sense the wonderment of a child.

—Mary Summer Rain

Love it the way it is.

—Thaddeus Golas

If you love life, do not squander time.
That is the stuff life is made of!

—JoeAnn Ludwig

ugh & Learn

Follow your dreams and
make the most of every experience.
—David Stern

The one fact I would
cry from every housetop is this—
the good life is waiting for us—
here and now!
—D. F. Skinner

Good old days start
with good new days like today.
—Denise Settle

Live, Love, I

Do not wait for life.
Do not long for it. Be aware,
always and at every moment, that the
miracle is in the here and now.

—Marcel Proust

Choose to be happy.
It is a way of being wise.

—Colette

Believe in yourself and in everything you
can be…not only will you be happy, but you
will be able to appreciate the good qualities
of the people around you.

—James Garner

We are all affecting the
world every moment, whether
we mean to or not. Our actions and
states of mind matter, because we're so
deeply interconnected with one another.

—Ram Dass

The human heart, at whatever age, opens
only to the heart that opens in return.

—Maria Edgeworth

There is always something left to love.
And if you ain't learned that,
you ain't learned nothing.

—Lorraine Hansberry

Live, Love, L

If you want others to be happy,
practice compassion; if you want to
be happy, practice compassion.

—Mary Stewbeck

We all live with the objective
of being happy; our lives are all
different and yet the same.

—Anne Frank

Thousands of candles can be
lighted from a single candle, and the
life of the candle will never be shortened.
Happiness never ceases by being shared.

—Chinese Proverb

augh & Learn

People who deal with life
generously and large-heartedly go
on multiplying relationships to the end.

—Arthur Christopher Benson

The faces of the people you love are
not going to be the same in the morning,
and neither is yours. Don't miss them.

—Leo Buscaglia

Treasure this day, and treasure yourself.
Truly, neither will ever happen again.

—Ray Bradbury

Live, Love, L

It is the experience of living that is
important, not searching for meaning.
We bring meaning by how we love the world.

—Bernie Siegel, M.D.

That is happiness; to be dissolved
into something complete and great.

—Willa Cather

You will recognize your own path when
you come upon it, because you will
suddenly have all the energy and
imagination you will ever need.

—Jerry Gillies

Being yourself is not remaining
what you were, or being satisfied with
what you are. It's a point of departure.

—Sydney Harris

The vision that you glorify in
your mind, the ideal that you enthrone
in your heart—this you will build
your life by, this you will become.

—James Allen

I now see my life, not as the slow shaping
of achievement to fit my preconceived
purposes, but as the gradual discovery
of a purpose which I did not know.

—Joanna Field

Live, Love, I

The whole secret of a
successful life is to discover
your destiny, and then do it.

—Henry Ford

Dedicate your life to a cause greater
than yourself, and your life will become
a glorious romance and adventure.

—Mack Douglas

I think the purpose of life is to be useful,
responsible, honorable, compassionate.
It is, above all, to matter: to count,
to stand for something, to have made
some difference that you lived at all.

—Leo Rosten

augh & Learn

Follow your desire
as long as you live.
—Ptah-Hotep

There is no happiness,
but there are moments of happiness.
—Spanish proverb

Take spring when it comes and rejoice.
Take happiness when it comes, and rejoice.
Take love when it comes, and rejoice.
—Carl Ewald

Live, Love, L

These are the magic years…
and therefore magic days…
and therefore magic moments.

—Anonymous

For all of us, the key is to pay
close attention to which activities make
us feel most alive and in love with life—
and then try to spend as much time as
possible engaged in those activities.

—Nathaniel Branden, Ph.D.

I have found that if you love life,
life will love you right back.

—Arthur Rubinstein

Starting each day I shall try
to learn something new about me and
about you and about the world I live in,
so that I may continue to experience all
things as if they have been newly born.

—Leo Buscaglia

Life has to be lived, that's all there is to it.

—Eleanor Roosevelt

Happiness is the only good.
The place to be happy is here.
The time to be happy is now.

—Robert Ingersoll

Live, Love, L

One day at a time—this
is enough. Live in the present
and make it so beautiful that it
will be worth remembering.

—Ida Scott Taylor

Don't run through life so fast that
you forget where you've been and lose
where you're going. Life is not a race,
but a journey to be savored every
step of the way.

—Kobi Yamada

You're only here for a short visit.
Don't hurry, don't worry. And be sure to
stop and smell the flowers along the way.

—Walter C. Hagen

Know the true value of time;
snatch, seize, and enjoy every moment of it.

—Philip Dormer Stanhope

The rainbow is more beautiful
than the pot at the end of it, because
the rainbow is now. And the pot never
turns out to be quite what I expected.

—Hugh Prather

I'd been busy, busy, so busy, preparing
for life, while life floated by me,
quiet and swift as a regatta.

—Lorence Cary

Live, Love, L

I'd rather be sorry for something
I did than for something I didn't do.

Only when we are no longer afraid
do we begin to live in every experience,
painful or joyous, to live in gratitude for
every moment, to live abundantly.

In masks outrageous and austere, the
years go by in single file. But none
has merited my fear, and none has
quite escaped my smile.

Laugh & Learn

It is not how much we
have, but how much we enjoy,
that makes happiness.

—Charles Spurgeon

Just think how happy you'd be
if you lost everything and everyone
you have right now…and then,
somehow got them back again.

—Kobi Yamada

That is what learning is. You suddenly
understand something you've understood
all your life, but in a new way.

—Doris Lessing

Live, Love, L

Those who are afraid to ask
are afraid to learn.

—Proverb

If you are willing,
great things are possible to you.

—Grenville Kleiser

No one but yourself can make your
life beautiful. No one can be pure,
honorable and loving for you.

—J.R. Miller

Don't seek to follow in the footsteps
of the wise. Seek what they sought.

—Basho

The art of living does not consist
in preserving and clinging to a particular
mode of happiness, but in allowing
happiness to change its form without
being disappointed in the change;
happiness, like a child, must be
allowed to grow up.

—Charles Morgan

Be willing to relinquish the life
you've planned, so as to have the
life that is waiting for you.

—Joseph Campbell

What a wonderful life I've had.
I only wish I'd realized it sooner.

—Colette

All my life there's been one
little rule that has worked wonderfully
for me: If there's any area of your life
in which you are less than 50 percent
happy, make an immediate change.

—Mick Carlson, age 87

I've learned it's usually the little things
that make a difference.

—John Gray, Ph.D.

augh & Learn

How we spend our days is,
of course, how we spend our lives.

—Annie Dillard

How simple it is to see
all the worry in the world cannot
control the future. How simple it is
to see that we can only be happy now,
and that there will never be a time
when it is not now.

—Gerald Jampolsky

Never lose your sense of wonder.

—Joe Batten

Live, Love, L

There is no end.
There is no beginning.
There is only the infinite
passion for life.

—Federico Fellini

Remember this—
that very little is needed to
make a happy life.

—Marcus Aurelius

How beautiful it is to be alive!

—Henry Septimus Sutton

Also available from Compendium Publishing are these spirited
and compelling companion books of great quotations.

Be the Difference

Because of You™
Celebrating the Difference
You Make™

Brilliance™
Uncommon Voices From
Uncommon Women™

Commitment to Excellence™
Celebrating the Very Best

Expect Success

Everyone Leads™
It takes each of us to make a
difference for all of us

Forever Remembered™
A Gift for the Grieving Heart™

I Believe in You™
To your heart, your dream and
the difference you make

Little Miracles™
To renew your dreams, lift your
spirits, and strengthen your resolve™

Reach for the Stars™
Give up the Good to
Go for the Great

Thank You
In appreciation of you,
and all that you do

To Your Success™
Thoughts to Give Wings to
Your Work and Your Dreams™

Together We Can™
Celebrating the power of
a team and a dream™

Whatever It Takes™
A Journey into the Heart
of Human Achievement™

You've Got a Friend™
Thoughts to Celebrate
the Joy of Friendship™

These books may be ordered directly from the publisher
(800) 914-3327. But please try your bookstore first!
www.compendiuminc.com